NOW & LATER

Social Skills for Today's Youth

Abstract

An Eight Week Program discussing the various social skills needed for now and later. This program will help student learn how to be socially responsible at home, in the classroom and amongst strangers. Social Skills help to promote positive behaviors in students so that they can become socially responsible citizens in their various walks of life.

Stephen J. Palmer

How To Use This Curriculum

This curriculum serves as a guide to help you as the facilitator and your students learn about the basic social skills used in today's society. Each lesson is geared toward learning new information and skill sets that can be easily practiced and used today. Be sure to add any new ideas and concepts that you may have in order to make this curriculum your own and tailor it for the specific needs of your students. Once your students begin to discuss the questions and participate in the lessons, they can begin to grasp the knowledge necessary to make them efficient and effective at communicating and interacting within today's society.

INTRODUCTION

RESPECT YOUR SELF

WHO DO I INTERACT WITH

NON-VERBAL VS. VERBAL COMMUNICATION

PROPER HYGIENE

ACCEPTING CRITICISM

EDUCATION & LEARNING

"Now & Later" Social Skills

Class Title

Instructor Notes

"Introduction to Class"

Make this class as fun as possible. Get each student excited about being a part of the class show how fun it is to learn about Social Skills.

Key Objectives

Students will be introduced to the Program and Instructor(s)

Students will introduce themselves and prepare for the next lesson.

Introductions

Introduce yourself by answering the bullets below and have each student follow in your stead by standing in front of the class or at their desks and introducing themselves.

• First and Last Name

• Grade or Age (for the instructor you can state what school you went to)

• Where you are from?

• Two Interesting things about yourself and

• What are you plans after high school?

Expectations and Class Rules

Class Expectations: (read aloud to the students)

• You can expect to have fun but in order to do so you must do the following:

• Be respectful to the instructor and other classmates

• Do not talk about or talk while someone else is speaking

• Pay attention and participate in the class

• And above all have Fun!!

"Now & Later" Social Skills

"What are Social Skills"

This lesson will always be your rubric and reference throughout the course. Continue to reiterate the definitions and steps in order to help students fully grasp what social skills are and how to use them.

Key Objectives

Students will learn what Social Skills

Students will learn how we use Social Skills in everyday living

Students will learn the advantages of proper Social Skills

Defining Social Skills

Social skills are the skills we use to **communicate and interact with each other**, both verbally and non-verbally, through gestures, body language and our personal appearance. (Adopted from skillsyouneed.com)

Three Things You Are Communicating:

1. Your Thoughts – This is what you are thinking.
If someone asks you "What do you think about this?" Can you properly communicate what you are thinking?

2. Your Messages – This is how you want to say something.
If your friend asks you, "How should I tell my mother about breaking her dish?" Can you help them create a message by communicating to them what they should say?

3. Your Feelings – This is how you feel.
Believe it or not, people do not know how you feel until you tell them. Can you explain to someone how you are feeling; if you are sad, mad, hurting,

Ways We Communicate:
Ask the Students if they can name the different ways we communicate today.

• Verbally: Words & Sounds

• Non-Verbally: Body Language & Expression (facial expression, gestures, and posture)

• Touch: This is part of using your senses (a hug, a slap of the hand, and punch out of anger)

Ways We Interact:

Calls	Mail	Email	Text Messages
Letters	Pictures	Videos	Sounds

Advantages of Good Social Skills

Good social skills can be learned and you should make sure that you learn them. Here are some advantages of having good social skills:

• More and Better Relationships

• Better Communication

• Career Advancement

• Higher Grades

• Overall Happiness

Ask the Students if they think the list above are advantages and why. Ask them if they can think of any other advantages not listed.

Discussion Questions

1. What are social skills?
2. What are the three ways we communicate?
3. What professional jobs are out there that deal with communication?

Takeaways

Ask Students to write down the following and bring to the next class:

A. When was a time you had good communication and interaction with someone that let to something good/positive happening for you?

B. When was a time you had bad communication and interaction with someone and it let to something bad/negative happening for you?

"Now & Later" Social Skills

Class Title   **"Respect Yourself"**

Class Subsection   What Do I Think About Myself?

Key Objectives

Students will learn about self-confidence

Students will learn how to overcome shyness

Think About This Quote

"Whether you think you can, or you think you can't – you are right." –Henry Ford
<u>Go around the room and ask each student what they think about the above quote.</u>

- What do you think Henry Ford meant by this?

- Who is the person that must think? (The Answer: "You")

- What two ways can this person think? (The Answer: "They Can or They Can't")

What do you think about yourself? Do you think that you can learn social skills or do you think that you can't? Whatever you choose to believe you are right. You are the only one that can think for you. You must decide that you can learn social skills and not allow others or even your own feeling get in the way.

Overcoming Shyness with Self-Confidence

Ask the Students how many of them would are shy? Ask them how many of them get nervous speaking to a crowd or around other people?

Do not worry if you get shy or if you are an introvert. Most people are afraid to talk in front of other people especially if they do not know them. Some people start to sweat, mumble their speech, shake, stutter their words, look away, or may not say anything at all.

However, if you need to communicate and interact with someone but get nervous it can cause you to miss out on many of the advantages that we discussed in our previous lesson. You must learn to have self-confidence and overcome the shyness when it comes to communicating and interacting with others.

<u>Read the questions and answers from the below picture aloud to the students and ask if any of them have ever felt like the person asking the questions or answering the questions.</u>

Q. Why am I afraid of people?
A. They would make fun of me or ask me scary questions.
Q. Are you a 'fortune teller' that you can tell it for sure?
A. No, I am not but they may ask me some questions I wont have answer to.
Q. So you are saying 'They may ask you' it means you were not sure the first time. So when you were not sure the first time how come you can be sure that you wont have answers to their questions? Even if you wouldn't have answer to those questions, why the F*** would that be a problem?
A. Because this has happened to me several times and I just froze.
Q. A lot of people don't know how to talk properly, people with weird laughter, making stupid comments, etc. So what if that happened to you? Would sky fall down on you?
A. I would feel embarrassed.
Q. Why would you feel embarrassed?
A. Because people would think what a stupid person I am.
Q. Again, Can you read peoples minds?
A. No. But if they did what would I do?
Q. Why would that be a problem?
A. They will make fun of me and tell others too that what a loser I am.
Q. Again its 'Mind reading', you cant read people's minds. OK why would that be a problem?
A. No one would talk to me and they will see me with weird looks.
Q. Are you sure that no one would talk to you? Are you sure there would be no one who will love you? Even if this happens, Why would that be a problem?
A. I will become alone.
Q. There are so many things which you done alone like playing computer games, watching movies alone, eating food alone, did you never enjoy doing those things alone?

An example of **Cognitive Behavioral Therapy** which was introduced by David Burns M.D and Professor at Stanford University.

This excerpt was taken from Dr. David Burns who is Professor at Stanford University. It shows how we often create our own fears and apprehensions when it comes to communicating or interacting with new people.

Discussion Questions

1. Why are some things that hold you back from communicating and interacting with other people?

2. If you could meet one person in the world dead or alive who would you meet and why?

3. Would you be afraid to speak to them if you only had one opportunity? Why or why not?

Takeaways

Ask Students to write down the following and bring to the next class:

A. What ways have being shy or not communicating or interacting with someone cause you to miss out on an opportunity or something good?

B. Introduce yourself to three people at your school, church, or recreational locations that you do not know and tell us about who you met.

Class Title	**"Respect Yourself"**
Class Subsection	What Do I Think About Others?

Key Objectives

Students will learn how to properly think about others

Students will learn how to use listening skills to help them better communicate and show respect to others

The Golden Rule

"Treat other as you would like to be treated"

<u>Ask students have they ever been mistreated or felt like they were? Ask them why do they feel that they were mistreated?</u>

Do you recall a time when you were mistreated? You probably did not like it or ever want it to happen again. No matter what the reason was what you felt was not something you probably want to feel again. Take that same feeling you and think about this: When you do not use proper social skills you can easily offend others and make them feel the same way you felt if not worse.

Just like you did not like feeling mistreated or being mistreated you must learn how to properly communicate and interact with others so that you do not make them feel the way you once felt.

Learn to Listen

Listening is the ability to correctly receive and interpret messages while communicating and interacting with others. If you do not listen you can miss what is being said, how it is being said and the opportunity to ask the proper questions to learn why something was said.

Listening is a major component to the communicating with others. If you do not correctly listen you can:

• Completely miss what was said

• Misunderstand what is was said and

• Cause tension between the person speaking and yourself because of a lack of respect for not listening.

How to Listen

Believe it or not we listen in two ways:

1. With our ears – through sounds

2. With our eyes – through sight.

You cannot properly listen to someone if you are talking while they are talking. If you cover your ears while someone is talking, more than likely you will miss what they are saying. The best way to respect someone is to listen to them while they are speaking. You listen by looking them in the eye while they speak and listening to their words as they speak.

Here are some Skills of Listening:

1. Stop Talking

2. Prepare Yourself to Listen

3. Make the Person Speaking Feel Comfortable

4. Remove Distractions (cellphone)

5. Be Patient and let them Speak

Discussion Questions

1. When was a time that you were ignored while you were speaking?

2. Did you feel disrespected when you were speaking and the person(s) you were speaking to were not listening?

3. How have you shown signs of disrespect to others by not listening?

Takeaways

Ask Students to write down the following and bring to the next class:

1. Choose two people young and old and ask them to tell you about their most exciting day. Be patient and listen to them as they speak not interrupting them and left them know that you appreciate them for sharing their story when they have finished.

Class Title	**"Respect Yourself"**
Class Subsection	Why We Must Get Along

Key Objectives

Students will learn about why people do not get along

Students will learn why it is important to get along with others

We are All Different

Believe it or not, you are a part of a group. The group is called Homo sapiens or humans. Within this group you belong to other subgroups. <u>Ask students to name some different subgroups</u>. Below are some examples:

• Race (ethnicity)

• Region (where you live)

• Religion (Christian, Muslim, Buddhist, etc.)

• Education (College or University)

• Grade (Freshmen, Junior, Sophomore, or Senior)

• Economic Status (how much money you make or have)

The same subgroups or things that make us different from other groups and create prejudices that may cause many people not to get along. We begin this section by saying we are all humans and it is that link that ties us all together.

No matter the different subgroups or differences we all share the common thread of being human and living on this planet. It is for this reason that we must all strive to get along and work together to not only take care of our planet but of each other.

Let's be honest. There are some people who make not like you because of your subgroup and there may be some people that you may not like because of their subgroup. For whatever reason we can all say that we have pre-judged someone at a particular time based on their subgroup. Pre-judging someone is wrong and not a sign of good social skills.

You have to learn how to not judge other just like you would not like to them to judge you. You must take the time to learn how to communicate and interact with various subgroups not matter the difference. Each person is just as important as the other. And when we learn to work together we can get along to become an effective team.

Be a Team Player

A team is separate individuals coming forming a group in order to work together in achieving a common goal. Whether that goal is to win a championship, build a building, grow a business, or pass grade, a team is a group of people that working together regardless of their difference to achieve their goal. <u>Ask the Students how many of them have ever been on a team. Ask them to name what their team did and what was their common goal.</u>

Group Activity

Have the students break into even group. Tell the group to name two things that make each member in the group different from the other and name one thing three things that they have in common. And how can the differences and similarities be helpful for each member. Have each group present in front of the class.

Discussion Questions

1. Have you ever worked with anyone that may have been different only to find that you have a lot in common?

2. What made you think that they were different?

3. How did you find out that you had things in common?

Takeaways

Ask Students to write down the following and bring to the next class:

A. Meet someone that is from a different subgroup from you and discuss that meeting at the next class.

"Now & Later" Social Skills

Key Objectives

Students will learn who they interact with at home

Students will learn the importance of interaction with family

Family

The first place you learn about Social Skills is within our home. The family that you are a part of has a major role in shaping the ways you think, act, interact and communicate. Before you ever step foot into a school or a new job, you were a member of a family. Families are not just made up of blood relatives but may be made of adoptive members, step children and other extended family. Below are a list of different family members. Have the students think about their relationships and the habits (whether good or bad) that they have picked up from one or more of these people.

Mom	Dad	Sister	Brother
Uncle	Aunt	Niece	Nephew
Grandma	Grandpa	Son	Daughter
Cousin	Husband	Wife	Stepparents

How you communicate and interact with those listed above have can play a major role on how you interact with others outside of your family.

How Do You Get Along

It is never too late to correct any problems at home. You should make an effort to try to communicate and interact with your family every day, even it is for five minutes. Some family members may not live with you so it may be hard to communicate every day, but you can try to at least speak to them on a monthly basis.

Here are some fun ways families can learn to get along and grow stronger relationships. Ask the Students can they think of any more.

- Eat dinner together

- Play Games together

- Travel Together

- Spend time talking with one another

- Send funny text messages to one another

- Take pictures

Discussion Questions

1. In what ways has your family shaped the way you think, communicate and interact with other people?

Takeaways

Ask Students to write down the following and bring to the next class:

A. Think of a family member that you lost. What do you wish you could have said or done with them before they passed?.

Class Title

Class Subsection

"Who Do I Interact With?"

Interaction At School

Key Objectives

Students will learn who they interact with at school

Students will learn how to interact with the various people at school

At School

School is a place for you to learn and get an education. You not only learn your core subjects like Math, Science, History, and Literature, but you also learn to communicate and interact with people beyond your family. Within your school you are one of hundreds of other people walking up and down the halls. You see people who are tall, short, young, old, thin, round, light, dark, and a host of other different things.

Your school is a great place to practice the social skills you are learning here in this class. There a many different people in your school. Below is a list of a people who might be in your school every day or at least once a week. Can you name anymore?

Teachers	Students	Principle	Administrative Staff
Librarians	Volunteers	Parents	Custodial Engineer

Respecting Adults

You should always be respectful to everyone you meet especially those who are adults. Adults are much older than you and have lived a little longer than you have. Out of respect you listen to what they say and not talk back. Regardless if they say something that may make you upset, it is best to not say anything than to say something that is disrespectful.

Your Teachers and Administrative Staff are examples of the adults that you should especially show respect to. No matter if you do not like them or get along, you must remember that they are to help you learn. If you have a question, you should raise your hand and wait your turn. When you do speak you should speak clearly and not in a disrespectful manner. Below is a list of questions you may ask your teacher. How could you say this in a disrespectful manner and how can you say it in a respectful manner?

<u>Have the Students give you examples of not how not to speaking to the teacher and the proper ways to speak to the teacher. (Reiterate the keys we learned about listening and that they should practice raising their hand and waiting to be acknowledged.</u>

The Wrong Way: Um excuse miss "what's your face" I am going to the bathroom.
The Right Way: (Raising your hand) Excuse me Ms. Johnson. May I please go to the bathroom? COME UP WITH OTHER EXAMPLES WITH THE STUDENTS.

Discussion Questions

A. What would you do if you were a teacher and you had a student that was constantly being disruptive in your class? Explain your answer.

B. How would you react to a student being disrespectful to you if you were the principle? Explain your answer.

Takeaways

Ask Students to write down the following and bring to the next class:

1. Write a thank you letter to one teacher and an administrator at your school. Think about something that you appreciate about them and put it in your letter.

"Now & Later" Social Skills

Class Title	**"Who Do I Interact With?"**
Class Subsection	Interactions at Work

Key Objectives

Students will learn who they interact with at work

Students will learn why it is important to have social skills at work

People at Work

When you are at work you are not only representing yourself but the brand, community and the company you work for. The way you communicate and interact with a variety of people can determine a lot of positive or negative outcomes. No matter the type of company you work for you will always have to deal with people. Here is a list of people that you might have to deal with.

- Co-Workers

- Boss

- Customers

- Vendors

The work you do and how you communicate can help to advance your further in your company or even get you fired.. The choice is yours whether or not you will learn to use the proper social skills at work.

Dealing with a Difficult Customer

Let's say that you are at work on the register and a customer with a bad attitude comes in and complains. How would you deal with them? Have the Students discussed ways that they would deal with the customer. (You may have to present them with a specific scenario to get the conversation started.)

The best way to deal with a difficult customer is to:

- Remain calm and do not raise your voice.

- Ask the customer what they would like you to do about the situation.

- Tell the customer you apologize for any problems or issues and that you will try to do everything you can within your policy in order to help them.

- Contact your immediate supervisor or manager to approve any refunds and have them deal with the issue if assistance is need.

The Importance of Good Social Skills at Work

You may not know it but your ability to communicate and interact with other effects more than just you others who are directly and indirectly connected to you and the company you work for. Here are some things that can be affected by your communication and interactions at work.

- Your Paycheck

- Your Job

- Relationships with Customers

- The Business as a Whole

- The Community you service

Have the Students discuss how each of the above bullets are affected and ways that they can help to positively affect them.

Discussion Questions

1. When was there a time you had to deal with a difficult co-worker? How did you handle it and what become of your actions?

2. You are the manager of a local food store and you told your staff to put the oranges in one section of the store. When your regional manager comes in he tells you that the oranges need to be on the other side of the store. How would you tell your staff who worked all day to move the oranges that they need to move them again?

Takeaways

Ask Students to write down the following and bring to the next class:

A. Where do you work and how do you deal with customers?

B. To you, is the customer always right?

"Now & Later" Social Skills

Class Title	**"Who Do I Interact With"**
Class Subsection	Recreation & Leisure Interactions

Key Objectives

Students will learn how to deal with strangers

Students will learn ways to be friendly

Dealing with Strangers

There are a lot of place that you may go to that you do not know people. You can travel to the mall, grocery store, on vacation, to the movies, and so many other places that we would not have enough time to list. When you go to these places you may go with close friends but the people who are there as well you do not know. How do you interact with them? Do you get nervous, scared or shy around strangers?

A stranger is a person that you do not know. With that being said, your friends were strangers before you even knew them.

"A Friend is only a stranger that you have grown to know and love." – Stephen J. Palmer

There are times you will have to communicate and interact with perfect strangers. Can you think of when some of those times might be? Here is are a few listed below:

- Saying excuse me while you are trying to get to your seat in the movie theatre.
- Going to a fast food restaurant to order food and talking the person taking your order.
- Seeing someone drop something out of their purse or wallet and telling them that they dropped it.

No matter the location or the event you will have to deal with strangers. If you want to be effective in your social skills you must learn how properly communicate and interact with strangers…You never know, a stranger can turn into a longtime friend!

Making New Friends

You may be surprised that once you learn to communicate and interact with different people, you may start to like their personality and develop friendships. Friends can come in many different shapes and sizes. They can be a part of one or several of the subgroups we discussed in the earlier class. The first thing you must do if you want make new friends is show yourself to be friendly. Here are some tips to make new friends.

- Smile

- Be Kind

- Don't be too loud

- Laugh

- Give Real Compliments

- Listen (use the skills we learned earlier) and

- Be Encouraging

The list above may seem easy but you would be surprised to find that many people have a difficult time practicing this list. You have to make an effort to show yourself friendly and practice these skills daily. As you begin to do these things, you will see that your new friends and even old friends will appreciate you more and probably start to mimic after you.

Discussion Questions

1. Think of your best friend. How did you all become friends? What made you want to be their friend?

2. Have you ever met a stranger that was friendly to you? How were they friendly?

Takeaways

Ask Students to write down the following and bring to the next class:

A. Choose two friends and ask them why they enjoy being your friend.

B. Ask them how you can be a better friend.

"Now & Later" Social Skills

Class Title	**"Non-Verbal vs. Verbal Communication"**
Class Subsection	What I Say

Key Objectives

Students will learn the difference between non-verbal and verbal communication

Students will learn the importance of watching what you say and how you say it.

Non-Verbal vs. Verbal Communication

Communicating with others makes up a large portion of our daily interactions with people. The things we say and the things we do not say play a major role in our how effective our social skills are. When it come communicating there are two forms that we use are non-verbal and verbal communication. Each form is important and can work together to help us become better communicators with people.

Below are the two type of communications:

• <u>Nov-Verbal</u>: gestures, posture and everything that consists of your body making movements while you speak or all by themselves. Non-verbal communication is communicating without words.

• <u>Verbal</u>: spoken words and sounds that come out of your mouth when you are communicating or through interactions. Can happen face-to-face, over the phone, through video or live chat.

One form is not more important than the other. Though you may only think that talking is important, what you do not say can either help or harm what you are saying. Think of it this way: Have you ever talked to someone and as they were talking you noticed that they were saying one thing but their gestures were doing another? This is an example of your non-verbal communication harming your verbal. You want to be sure the get a grasp on what you are saying without your words. This encompasses what it means to have great social skills.

What I Say

We have all heard the phrase, "If you don't have anything nice to say, do not say anything at all." This is very true when it comes to communicating and interacting with others. People tend not to like people who make them feel bad or talk bad. People who

• People who complain about everything

• People constantly compare

• People who are constantly blaming other

• People who are competing with others

• People who do not have anything nice to say

You may know some people like this or may wish you did not know them. Either way, most people do not want to be around people who are always talking negative. This is why it is important that you watch what you say even if you are angry, tire, frustrated, or confused. You cannot be known someone with great social skills if you are known as the person that talks negatively. Be careful what you say to family, friends, and strangers…If you don't have anything nice to say, do not say anything at all.

Discussion Questions

1. Can you think of a time that you wish you did not say something that you said or someone said something to you that you wish they did not say to someone? How did it make you feel? What become of that person or you?

Takeaways

Ask Students to write down the following and bring to the next class:

A. Make it a point to tell at least 3 of your friends something nice and special about them. Practice watching what you say and have your family or friends help hold you accountable.

"Now & Later" Social Skills

Class Title

"Non-Verbal vs. Verbal Communication"

Class Subsection

How I Say It

Key Objectives

Students will learn the importance of tone in your voice when speaking

Tone of Voice

Your tone involves the pitch, volume and inflections in your voice while you speak. Usually you can tell by someone's tone how they are feeling or the type of emotion they are going through. Here is a fun activity that you can do to better understand tone. Have three students come up and have them turn their back toward the class. Give each student one of the bullets below and have them say the phrase listed and see if the other students can guess by their tone what emotion it is.

• Excited: "Did you see that car that just drove by?"

• Angry: "I wish they would stop knocking on my door!"

• Sad: "I'm sorry that I missed your party."

By listening to the tone in a person's voice you can often tell when someone is excited, angry, sad, scared or even bored. The tone in which you speak is very important in communicating with people in your family, school and recreational play. Practice you can tell by the volume and pitch in their voice. If someone is sad or even bored you can

Class Activity

Ask the Students the Following Questions:

• Why do think tone is important when communicating?

• Is tone more important than the words you say?

• What do you think the following quote means: "It's not just what you say, it is how you say it?

Discussion Questions

1. Have you ever talked to someone whose tone made you feel disrespected or made you upset? Explain.

"Now & Later" Social Skills

Class Title	**"Non-Verbal vs. Verbal Communication"**
Class Subsection	Body Language

Key Objectives

Students will learn how to use proper body language and demonstrate ways to do so

Body Language

Body Language are the gestures a person's face or body (arms, hands, eyebrows, shoulders, etc.) make when they are communicating and interacting. Body language communicates a message without a person having to use words. How often have you had to communicate with someone but could they could not hear you or you had to use gestures to help them understand what you were saying? Have you ever been in a situation like that? <u>Allow the Students to answer and explain.</u>

When you are communicating with others who are looking at you, you need to be very careful that your body language is not giving off a different message from what you are saying. If this happens to be the case, the people you are talking with can become confused and get mixed messages. Here are some examples of gestures that you probably use and did not know was sending a message.

• Posture (how you are sitting. If you are sloughing sitting up straight, etc.)

• Looking away when someone is talking to you.

• Lowering your head

• Nodding your head for "No" and Shaking your head for "Yes"

• Hands on your hips

Whatever gesture you use whether you know it or not is giving off a message. If you want to be sure that you are conveying the right message be careful in the body language you use.

Class Activity

Break the class up into two separate team. Designate a captain for each group and make that person the spokesperson for their team. Give each captain four (8) sheets of blank paper for which they must write their answer. Toss a coin to see who will go first. The first team will send one representative from their group up and they must act out of the word that you will give them from the list below without using any words or sounds. Each team will have 30 seconds to write their answer down and present it to you when you call time. The team that gets the answer right wins a point. The team with the most points wins! (The parenthesis are just some examples of ways they can act out their word).

• Hungry (rub their stomach)

- Tired (yawn)

- Angry (stop feet or fold arms)

- Sick (pretend they are regurgitating)

- Not Listening (hands over ears)

- Wait of Minute (hold finger up)

- Confused (palms up shrug shoulders)

Discussion Questions

1. Have you ever experienced a time when someone came up to you and asked you a question based on your body language? What gesture or posture did you have that made them think that you felt some type of way?

2. When a friend is feeling a particular way can you tell by their body language? How so? Explain your answer.

Takeaways

Ask Students to write down the following and bring to the next class:

A. Observe your friends and families body language. What did their body language say without them having to open their mouth?

"Now & Later" Social Skills

Class Title	**"Proper Hygiene"**
Class Subsection	My Body My Odor

Key Objectives

Students will learn what proper hygiene and why it is important.

What is Hygiene

Hygiene are clean habits that help to maintain health and help prevent the spreading of diseases (germs) from you and to you from others. In order to have good personal hygiene you must practice healthy habits when it cleaning body, mouth, clothes and the area in which you live, learn, and work. Proper hygiene promotes:

• Health and Wellness

• And Cleanliness

Why Is Hygiene Important

Have you ever spoken to someone and their breath was not fresh or they may have just come from the gym so they smelled and looked sweaty? Just like people do not like talking to a person that is negative the same is true for a person who has poor hygiene. It is considered rude and disrespectful is you have a foul odor and try to hold a conversation with them. Of course there are instances when you cannot help that you just came from the gym or the person you are talking to is just as sweaty, but what we are talking about is in your everyday conversation.

Just as much as people do not want to be around someone that has an odorous smell the same is true for someone that has too much cologne or perfume on. When people put on too much cologne or perfume it can become overbearing and be just as bad as not smelling good.

Having good hygiene is a form of non-verbal body language that can either draw people to you or away from you.

Discussion Questions

1. What is your favorite brand of perfume or cologne? Why is it your favorite?

2. Have you ever been around someone that smelled really bad or had too much cologne or perfume? How do you handle your interaction with them?

"Now & Later" Social Skills

"Proper Hygiene"

Tips & Techniques

Key Objectives

Students will learn several proper hygiene practices that they can utilize everyday

Good Personal Hygiene

We have already discussed what hygiene is, so now we will look at some good hygiene tips. These tips can help you stay fresh and healthy throughout the day, as well as add a positive touch to your social skills through non-verbal messages.

• Taking a shower at least once a day when able and/or after sweating.

• Brushing your teeth at least once or after every meal.

• Washing your hair at least once a week to get any germs out.

• Washing your hands after you use the bathroom, before you eat or have touched a common area.

• Changing into clean clothes and washing the ones that get dirty.

• Turning away from people when you cough or sneeze and covering your mouth with tissue.

• Putting on lotion and deodorant after you have showered.

• Avoid shaking hands while you are eating, if you are sick or have touched something dirty.

• Always carry mints or gum to keep your breath fresh

No matter if you are male or female it is important to always stay fresh and practice good hygiene. As you practice these good personal hygiene tips you will find that it will become easier to follow and do so that you will form good habits that will help boost your social skills and self-esteem.

Discussion Questions

1. Ask the Students about the various products such as toothpaste, soap, deodorant, etc. that they may use or wanted to try?

"Now & Later" Social Skills

Class Title	**"Proper Hygiene"**
Class Subsection	Healthy Sweat

Key Objectives

Students will learn the importance of exercise and fitness

Healthy Sweat

It is good for you sweat especially when you are participating in a healthy fitness/exercise routine. Physical activity such as exercise and fitness helps you to (1) Stay active (2) helps you to concentrate during learning; and (3) keeps your body healthy and well. Having a consistent exercise routine increase your chances for a good mental and physically life. With so much technology, games and social media pulling your attention away from activities that require your physical movement, it is even more important that you create a healthy fitness/exercise routine so that you do not become stiff and unhealthy. Get started on it today!

Class Participation

Have the students create some room for everyone to move around. (You may have to move chairs or desks or even go outside for the portion). You will call out an exercise and each student must perform the exercise. (Feel free to add any other exercises or stretches that is doable for the students).

- Jumping Jacks

- Toe Raise/Calf Raises

- Running in Place

- Push-ups

- Lunches

- Various Stretches

Discussion Questions

1. Do you have consistent exercise routine? If so what kind of exercises do you do?

Takeaways

Ask Students to write down the following and bring to the next class:

A. Have each student create a simple workout plan/routine that they can follow throughout the week.

"Accepting Criticism"

Compliments vs. Criticism

Key Objectives

Students will learn the difference between a compliment and criticism

Compliments

A compliment is a remark that says something good about someone or something. The remark expresses admiration or approval. It is saying something nice and true about someone. Mark Twain said, "I can live for two months on a good compliment." Compliments are great ways to encourage and show respect for others. Compliments are healthy ways to communicate and interact with others. Here are few tips for giving compliments:

• Be Genuine: avoid you words like the "best" and phrases like "the most"

• Be Specific: I like those shoes vs. I like those green shoes how they accent your dress.

• Don't wait for the perfect moment. Share what you have then and there.

• Be Concise. Don't take a long time. A good compliment should not take too long to say.

• Don't expect anything in return. A compliment is meant to be given not to get something in return.

<u>Ask the Students when was the last time they gave someone a compliment that consisted on the bullets above.</u>

Criticism

Criticism is the verbally expressing disapproval or noting problems and faults in another person. Criticism can be a very touchy and uncomfortable experience. Here are some ways to give a criticism:

• Know the person. It is best if you know the person and have a prior relationship with them. This could make the whole process a lot easier.

• Know the reason. Why are you criticizing? Is it to help bring a positive change or just to let that person know? If you are not trying to help the person you are criticizing you should not give it.

• Avoid using selfish words and only think about yourself.

- Trying giving using what is called the PNP approach: Positive Negative Positive. This means you give start with a compliment or say something positive then the criticism then end with a positive compliment.

How to Receive Criticism

Receiving criticism can be just as hard if not more uncomfortable that giving criticism. Remember the goal of any criticism is supposed to help bring a positive change. Here are some tips for receiving criticism.

- Be quiet and listen to what they are saying.

- Ask helpful questions that get to the bottom of the issue.

- Refer back to the goals.

- Ask what changes you help make in order keep the issue from happening again.

Discussion Questions

Takeaways

Ask Students to write down the following and bring to the next class:

A. Give three people that you know compliments.

"Now & Later" Social Skills

Class Title

Class Subsection

"Accepting Criticism"

Why Do I Need It and How Do I React To It?

Key Objectives

Students will learn the importance of receiving criticism

Why Do You Need Criticism

Remember the goal of criticism is to bring a positive change in the person receiving it. Yes, it can be difficult to hear "not so good" things about yourself, but the purpose is to help you make a positive change and do something better. Here are a few reasons why you need criticism. <u>Ask the Students if they can think of anymore reasons and if they agree.</u>

• You get a different perspective

• Learn how others think about you

• Learn something that needs to change

• You learn how to deal with people.

If you want to effectively communicate and interact act with others you must learn how to take criticism.

How Do I React to Criticism

People who learn have to receive criticism can benefit from the list above and the positives that are associated with the reason why you need criticism above. Below are some ways to receive "constructive" criticism.

• *Keep silent and let the person speak* – You want be sure that you listen to each word and critique that they are giving so you can understand what needs to be corrected or change.

• *Do not interrupt them from speaking* – Even if you may not agree with what they are saying the best way to keep the conversation positive is to let them finish what they are saying them give feedback.

• *Do not take immediate offense* – Some things that are stated may offend you and cause you to become defensive. Respect what they are saying at the moment because they may not understand the reason why you did or did not do what you are stating.

• *Do not criticize them* – when responding to their criticism, only talk about the critique at hand avoiding the urge to talk about things that they may have done or not do. Keep the subject on you and you alone.

One of the best ways to avoid having to be criticized is to critique yourself. Learn to evaluate your actions, non-actions, attitude, tone, communication and interactions with others. If you know there are things that could be better and make a positive impact, by all means do. Us e this time to better yourself so no one else will have to.

Discussion Questions

1. Have you ever had to criticize or critique a family member, friend, or co-worker? How did you handle critiquing them? What was the result of your critique?

2. Recall a time when someone gave you constructive criticism. How did you feel during and after the criticism? What did you like about the way they critiqued you and what would you change about their approach?

Takeaways

Ask Students to write down the following and bring to the next class:

A. Critique yourself and pick two (2) areas in your life that you need to change. Write down your findings and how to make the needed changes in order to turn that area into a positive or personal success.

"Now & Later" Social Skills

Class Title	**"Education & Learning"**
Class Subsection	Knowledge is Power

Key Objectives

Students will learn the importance of education.

Knowledge is Power

You have probably often heard it said, "Knowledge is Power!" But do you really know what that means? This quote talks about the importance of education and learning. People who have been educated are in the "know". This means that they have an understanding about something and with that understanding they can do something with which they know. Think of it like this: If you know basic math (how to add, subtract, multiply, and divide) I can trust that you can count, so I can hire you to handle my inventory at my clothing shop because you "know" basic math.

Can you think of some things that you either learned from school or even online that can help you at your current job or in the future? Have the Students answer the question. Below are some examples.

• English (writing a receipt or taking an order at a restaurant)

• Reading (reading instructions on a new machine; a memo from a boss)

• History (when making a decision you can look back at those who made one before and learn from their mistakes or success)

• Geometry (helping someone move certain pieces through tight squeezed door)

Discussion Questions

1. What have you learned in school that you think that you may never use? Why do you think that you will never use it?

Takeaways

Ask Students to write down the following and bring to the next class:

A. Look up two job descriptions that you would be interested in working. Find out what things you need to know and learn in order to be hired for that job.

"Now & Later" Social Skills

Class Title	**"Education & Learning"**
Class Subsection	After High School

Key Objectives

Students will (begin) to decide their option for after high school.

After High School

Have you thought about what you are going to do when you have obtained your high school diploma? Once you graduate you will be free to decide on your options and the routes you want to take. Remember the decisions that you make today will effect tomorrow.

What are Your Options

You have several choices to choose from once you graduate, but the time to think about those choices are not when you graduation but before you graduate. You want to know where you are headed once you graduate before you graduate so that you can prepare yourself to do the work that is necessary to see your choice to the end. The great thing about your choice is that you can choose a variation of the following:

• College (4 or 2 year)

• Military

• Work

• Start a Business (Entrepreneurship)

<u>Discuss the options with the students and get their feedback of how and why they chose their particular option.</u>

Discussion Questions

1. Have you thought about life after school? What do you plan on doing after you graduate? Why do you want to do what you chose?

Takeaways

Ask Students to write down the following and bring to the next class:

A. Make a list of the three top college you want to go.

B. Make a list of your top three majors you would like to study at the schools you have chosen above?

Class Title	**"Education & Learning"**
Class Subsection	Be A Continual Learner

Key Objectives

Students will learn what a continual learner is and how to become one.

What is a Continual Learner

A Continual Learner is a lifelong learner. This is a person who continues to learn through voluntary and self-motivated pursuit of knowledge in order to better themselves personally and/or professionally.

A Continual Learner continues to learn to:

1. Better themselves

2. Better those around them and the company they work for.

3. Develop and new skill-set or trade

4. Adapt to changes in technology or practices in a particular field.

How to Become a Continual Learner

Here are some ways to determine if you are a continual learner. Ask the Students can they identify with any of the listed letters below. Discuss with them why they feel that one of the letters below represent them or why it does not represent them.

(adopted from www.talentlms.com)

A. Do you ask for help when you do not understand something?

B. Do you observe people who have more experience doing something than you do?

C. Do you try to figure out new ways to do a particular task or activity instead of always using the conventional way?

D. Do you practice what you have learned previously from those who taught you?

E. Do you take personal training courses or classes outside of your routine school hours?

If you could not answer 'yes' to any of the listed items above, all hope is not lost. You can begin to make these things habits for your life so that you can be on track to become a continual learner.

Read the following quote aloud to the students and have them tell you what they think:

"Our whole life is an Education – we are 'ever-learning,' every moment of time, everywhere, under all circumstances something is being added to the stock of our previous attainments. Mind is always at work once its operations commence. All men are learners,

whatever their occupation; in the palace, in the cottage, in the park, and in the field. These are the laws stamped upon Humanity." —Edward Paxton Hood, 1852

Discussion Questions

1. How often do you learn something new outside of school?

2. What do you think is more important, the information you learn in school or the lessons outside of school?

Takeaways

Ask Students to write down the following and bring to the next class:

A. Create a routine for learning. Whether it be read a new book every month or to learn a new language. Utilize the technology that you have through the internet and continue to learn.

Be sure to check out these other valuable resources from the TPH Group, LLC available on Amazon.com, Kindle and Google Books:

"The Pillars 4 Success"
How to Turn Knowledge into
Action and Action into Success.

"Stop! Continue…Start:
A Guide to Self-Evaluation"
Learn how to elevate your life by
evaluating your actions.

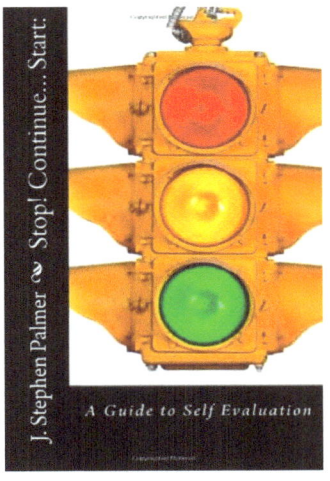

"5 Things Every Elite Athlete
Should Know About Sports"
If you want to be an elite player on and off the
field, you must learn these five principles that can
help to improve your game.

www.ingramcontent.com/pod-product-compliance
Lightning Source LLC
Chambersburg PA
CBHW060839290526
45792CB00006BB/1991